# TUCKER,
## THE TOO LOVABLE CAT

Also By Anna Marie Blumenstock

*Hugs, Kisses, and Wisdom*

*Cheyanne, The Miracle Dog*

# TUCKER,

## THE TOO LOVABLE CAT

ANNA MARIE BLUMENSTOCK

iUniverse, Inc.
Bloomington

# Tucker, the too lovable cat

iUniverse books may be ordered through booksellers or by contacting:

iUniverse
1663 Liberty Drive
Bloomington, IN 47403
www.iuniverse.com
1-800-Authors (1-800-288-4677)

ISBN: 978-1-4759-1431-3 (sc)
ISBN: 978-1-4759-1432-0 (ebk)

Printed in the United States of America

iUniverse rev. date: 04/16/2012

# Contents

# *Dedication*

Dedicated to my sweet mother.

# *Acknowledgments*

Thank you to Alicia, who found my dear Tucker.

Also to Barbara, Bob, Janice, John, Judy, and Vera, great cat lovers.

With special heartfelt thanks to Ginny and Philip Gonzalez
who have been an inspiration to me.

# CHAPTER 1

## *Circle of Life*

*"Until one has loved an animal, part of
one's soul remains unawakened."*
—*Anatole France*

There is an underlying linkage between all beings on this Earth. It has
been said that when a butterfly flaps its wings, it creates a tiny disturbance
that, if conditions are just right, can cause a weather change in another
remote location. This theory demonstrates the interconnectedness of life.
Every action we take, or don't take, has an impact on the lives of others—at
times, a world away.

From butterflies to earthworms, from bacteria to birds, all beings have
something precious to give; each has a perfect place in creation. All
animals carry within them a special song that makes them essential to the
orchestra of life. Earthworms are essential to life on Planet Earth. Without
their ability to burrow, which plows and aerates the soil, or their ability
to ingest soil and pass it through their bodies, which re-mineralizes it, the
topsoil would cease to exist and we would all die.

All things in nature are connected, and we humans did not weave the web
of life, but are merely strands of it and whatever we do to the web we do to
ourselves. We are not separate from the web of life but merely one strand
in the design. Animals may be the teachers who can help us recover that
sense of connection. In the animal as in the human there is a spirit that
responds and corresponds to the Great Spirit, whose life and breath are in
every being. Everything affects everything else in the entire universe in a
web-like manner. Positive thoughts and actions taken by one of us affect
everyone else. It is this interconnectedness that enables the circle of life.

If life means anything at all, if we beings are connected in any way spiritually, then somehow whatever we do to the least of us, the weakest and most helpless, we do also to ourselves.

There is a strong and unseen contact between all of humanity. Some Native Americans call this link 'the long body,' which is the belief that everyone is joined on a spiritual level. This means that people do not just exist within their own bodies. Rather, there is a link between self and others, or past and present, even life and death. For the Native Americans that meant that the tribe would all exist within the same web of experience for as long as the tribe existed.

North American Native nations understand this interconnectedness. They realize that individual contentment is based on the collective needs of all. This belief is the basis of everything they do in their daily activities and ensures harmony within their culture. The Native way of cooperation rather than competition was foreign to the Europeans who took over the Native land and tried to dominate their cultures. When the Europeans came to North America, they outlawed the spiritual beliefs of the Natives. What was viewed by the Europeans as a primitive and regressive culture was actually the direction in which we all must move to achieve global peace and sustainability.

Animals live in peace and dignity with nature. Animals pass through forests, mountains, and waterways without destruction. The American Indians were known for having a deep respect for land and animals. J. Allan Boone, the great-grandson of Daniel Boone, wrote a wonderful book entitled, <u>Kinship With All Life</u>. In this book he reasons that when a white man would meet a dangerous snake on a path, the snake would usually try to bite him, whereas if a snake met an Indian, the snake would do him no harm. Boone says this is because the snake can sense the thoughts of each individual. The white man is usually thinking something like, "Oh my gosh! A snake! I have to kill it before it kills me!" Whereas the Indian is thinking: "Greetings, my beautiful slivery friend. God bless you and may you have a delightful day." The snake senses these thought vibrations and responds accordingly. It is believed that some level of sixth sense is available to humans if we try to understand and bond with nature and open our eyes and ears to what nature has to teach. When there is love for animals and a willingness to learn and accept them as they are, our ability to understand them grows. The mind and heart open and expand. With time and openness, a deeper understanding and communication with animals is possible.

According to a Pawnee legend, a great council is held whenever a person seeks growth or spiritual counsel, or is in need of an animal friend. The council considers which animal would be best for that human being and sends the animal to that person. Sometimes it may be just a brief encounter, while walking along one sees an animal and feels better for it or receives an insight. Many times the animal sent is a stricken or helpless creature, to encourage the person to care for it. According to legend, this is why so many people who have taken in stray animals come to feel that the animal they almost did not rescue became the most precious being they know, and that the day they found this dear animal was the luckiest day of their lives. I am among one of these lucky people, for the day I rescued two dogs from an animal shelter, a cat from the humane society, and took in three starving stray cats changed my life forever.

The following words are over seven thousand years old from the Vedas, collections of sacred writings of ancient India.

## *Indra's Net*

*There is an endless net of threads throughout the universe.*
*The horizontal threads are in space.*
*The vertical threads in time.*
*At every crossing of threads there is an individual.*
*And every individual is a crystal bead.*
*The great light of absolute being illuminates*
*and penetrates every crystal being,*
*And every crystal being reflects not only the light from*
*every other crystal in the net, but also every reflection*
*of every reflection throughout the universe.*

# CHAPTER 2

## *Hero*

*"Even a cat is a lion in her own lair."*
—*Indian Proverb*

One sunny day while my father was fishing he noticed a helpless kitten in the middle of the river struggling in the tide. There had been rain the night before and the current was swift in the river. The tiny kitten was struggling to stay afloat against the swift current. My father being the loving hero that he was threw down his fishing rod, dived into the river, and quickly snatched up the traumatized kitten just in time.

Year's later history was to repeat itself when my dear friend, Vera, received a new black kitten. Her husband, Eric, found a helpless black kitten while fishing. The kitten jumped from a tree limb onto Eric's head, landing on his hat. The cat refused to move and dug his small needle-like claws into the hat. That day, Vera received a new kitten, which wasn't anything new for Vera, who dearly loved cats. Throughout her life she had several beloved cats. I remember before the death of her dear beloved cat, Pumpkin. Vera made a little bed over the floor register to keep her dear Pumpkin warm. So this new little black kitten brought in new life for Vera who deeply mourned the loss of her Pumpkin.

The tiny kitten my father saved was a tortoiseshell cat with beautiful green eyes. My father was already a hero in my eyes but when he came home that day with this beautiful tiny kitten he was not only my hero but my four sisters' hero as well. Our eyes grew larger and larger as my father told his tale of rescuing this darling little kitten. Our hero's, adventure would be revered and passed down through the generations.

My mother was already accustomed to my father bringing home lost and injured animals. Her house was full of pets—a dog, rabbits, parakeets, hamsters, turtles, and fish. One more pet would just mean more love in the house. But the kitten was destined to live with our next-door neighbors, Rose and John, who fell in love with the precious kitten at first glance. They named the kitten, Tooley.

My father's status as a hero would grow as our neighbors, Rose and John grew to love this little kitten. Rose and John had tried to have children for years with no luck and this little kitten filled a gap in their hearts.

Whenever I was playing outside, Tooley would come over to me. I just loved petting her and hearing her booming purr. So started my love affair with cats when I was four years old. But it would not be until four years later that we welcomed a pet cat into the family.

# CHAPTER 3

## *Sam Wong, #1 Son*

*"The smallest feline is a masterpiece."*
*—Leonardo Da Vinci*

For a wedding gift my sister, Mary, was given a beautiful blue eyed Siamese kitten. She and her new husband immediately fell in love with this soft, little, loving kitten. But much to her dismay Mary became deathly allergic to her new loving pet. Mary broke out with hives, watery eyes, and was short of breath. Brokenhearted she asked my parents to adopt a new pet into the family. I was filled with joy. My mother, who longed for a son after 5 daughters, named the new family member, Sam Wong, #1 Son. Sam Wong was silky soft with the most beautiful blue eyes. We all fell in love with Sam Wong and he soon became my parent's proud number one son.

There was a fish aquarium on our dining room table and Sam Wong loved to watch the fish swim around. He never tried to get the fish but his eyes grew bigger and bigger as he watch the fish swim around in their large tank. It was as if the fish were entertaining Sam Wong. He could sit for hours watching the fish. But maybe even more than the fish, Sam Wong loved to watch Ringo, our parakeet. Each morning I would wake up and sing to Ringo. He would chirp and tweet back to me. Sam Wong would watch our morning ritual and would tilt his head as Ringo and I sang. Then after roaming around the house for a while Sam Wong would go and watch the fish. Between the fish and Ringo he had quite a full day of entertainment.

Sometimes we would let Ringo out of his cage to fly around the house and get exercise. My mother would put Sam Wong in a bedroom and close the door. One day my sister did not realize that Ringo was out flying around and let Sam Wong out of the bedroom. Ringo was flying high around the living room and Sam Wong eyed him and started to chase after Ringo. Ringo landed on the fireplace mantel where my mother proudly displayed all her antiques. Sam Wong leapt up on the fireplace mantel and casually walked across the entire mantel. As each cherished antique fell in slow motion and crashed to the floor my mother's heart sank. My mother ran and tried to catch her antiques but missed as each one dropped.

My father caught Sam Wong and eventually Ringo flew back into his cage but my mother never recovered from losing her beloved antiques, all of which were family heirlooms. Thirty years later this event would still be a party conversation for my mother. After a while, I think she had more fun telling the story then gazing upon her antiques.

# CHAPTER 4

## *Cats, Cats, and More Cats*

*"No matter how much cats fight, there*
*always seem to be plenty of kittens."*
*—Abraham Lincoln*

Sam Wong, #1 Son brought years of joy to our family. Sam Wong was an in-door cat but one day he escaped out the back door and climbed up to the very top of a high tree in the backyard. My father climbed up the tree and safely brought my mother's number one son back into her arms. A few years later this episode would repeat, but my father was at work. My mother went outside to hang some laundry up on the close line when Sam Wong ran outside with her. Sam Wong was startled by a loud jet passing overhead and climbed high up in a tree in the far backyard. Mother went back and tried to coax him down but Sam Wong was terrified, and crying. Mom called the fire department and a fireman climbed up the tree and recovered Sam Wong. It was just like in the movies. Sam Wong, #1 Son was rescued again. Needless to say after that, we made sure Sam Wong did not escape from the house again.

Sam Wong was the first of a list of cats that would become my loving companions. Each cat had his or her own special charm as beloved family members. One such cat was Sheena. Sheena was a gray cat with piercing green eyes. She was a very delicate cat and small for her age. Every time someone came over and saw Sheena they thought she was just a kitten. Once when Sheena was 16 years old my neighbor dropped off some plants for me and noticed Sheena peeking around the corner at her. My neighbor asked, "Did you just get a kitten?" Much to her surprise I told her Sheena was 16 years old.

Another cat I had was B.B. B.B. stood for 'Bruce Blumenstock' but sometimes it stood for 'Bad Boy'. B.B. was such a rascal. He had a black goatee on his white face and looked just like a French cat poet or painter. B.B. liked to leap across rooms without touching the ground. He would get around the house by leaping from couch to table to chair. B.B. would get all around the house not walking on the floor but by leaping here and there. He would slide across coffee tables leaving a wake of books, magazine, and nick-knacks all over the floor. One day B.B. knocked over all my plants neatly arranged on my plant stand. Pots, soil and plants were scattered all over the living room floor. In the summer when B.B. was hot he would stretch out in the bathtub. One day I noticed that while B.B. was lying in the bathtub it looked like he was flying through the sky. I always told everyone how B.B. flew through the air around my house and never touched the ground. So I took a photograph of him lying in the bathtub. The photo looked just like B.B. was flying though the sky. I showed the photograph to my friends and we would get a big laugh out of it.

A friend of mine from work gave me the most darling Calico cat named Patches. Patches was the most loving cat. One day I heard her growling and hissing and could not believe my ears. "Could that be my precious Patches making those awful noises?" I asked myself. Running to see what was the problem I saw Patches stuck between the curtains and the venetian blinds. One paw was suck in the curtains and one paw was stuck between the venetian blinds. Patches was trying to get up to her perch and look outside. It took me a while to get her out of that mess. After that I made sure the curtains and blinds were not closed at the same time again.

Along with my love of cats was my deep love for dogs too. While growing up our family had the most elegant Irish Setter named Guenevere. Before Patches came into my life I had the most adorable dog named Ginger. One Thanksgiving my sister handed me a box that had written on it: SEARS SPECTRUM #2870287 SAE 10W-40 Motor Oil. My sister tricked me into thinking that there were really oil cans in the box, and when I opened up the box much to my surprise was the most adorable puppy. Ginger had golden hair with big brown eyes. She was part Collie and part Golden Retriever. Her eyes penetrated my eyes and I was never the same. Ginger became good friends with Sheena, B.B., and Patches not to mention my parent's dog CoCo. Ginger and CoCo soon became know as the Spice

Girls. They were inseparable. The Spice Girls didn't form their own band but they sure had a big fan club. Among one of their fans was Patches. Patches loved to be with CoCo and Ginger. She would sleep while they slept, Patches would eat when they ate, all three of them would play at the same time.

Days would fly into months and months into years and the love between all the pets grew and grew. Your heart is never the same when a pet dies; it is losing a part of you. I truly believe that pets find us. We are not their owners but rather their friends. Pets pick us and they choose to stay with us. Having a beloved pet also carries the responsibility of caring for them until the end of their life. It is hard to say goodbye but sharing a life with a beloved pet, no matter how short, is rewarding and worth the mourning rather than not having that special love.

Sheena and B.B died of old age. Old age had set into our beloved Spice Girls and arthritis took its toll. CoCo and Ginger died only a few days apart from each other. CoCo was 16 years old and Ginger was 12 years old but when I lovingly glanced at these two sweet dogs I remember them as puppies, years ago. CoCo nipping at my heels and Ginger nuzzling my face.

Patches loved Ginger. It was as if she knew when Ginger's time was coming to an end. Patches would stay by Ginger's bed and watch her sleep. Patches would sleep next to Ginger during her last few weeks. Patches always slept with me at night and I would awake in the middle of the night to find her watching over Ginger.

At Steere House Nursing and Rehabilitation center in Rhode Island there is a very unique cat that comforts dying patients. Steere House is so different from other nursing homes in that it has a menagerie of cats, rabbits, and birds. Among these furry friends is Oscar the cat. Oscar is a very special cat with an extraordinary gift. Oscar senses instinctively when the end of life is near. When it is a patient's last hours Oscar begins his vigil. As if on a mission from heaven he strides into a patient's room and curls up on their bed and begins his blessed vigil. When a patient is in their last hours Oscar gives comfort, tenderness, and companionship.

Just like Oscar, Patches stayed with Ginger in her last hours giving her love. Even after Ginger was gone Patches kept searching for her. I knew then and there that we were ready for another pet. Would it be a dog or cat? Or both!

## THE RAINBOW BRIDGE

*There is a bridge connecting heaven and Earth. It is called the Rainbow Bridge because of its many colors. Just this side of the Rainbow Bridge is a land of meadows, hills and valleys, all of it covered with lush green grass.*

*When a beloved pet dies, the pet goes to this lovely land. There is always food and water and warm spring weather. There, the old and frail animals are young again. Those who are maimed are made whole once more. They play all day with each other, content and comfortable.*

*There is only on thing missing. They are not with the special person who loved them on Earth. So each day they run and play until the day comes when one suddenly stops playing and looks up! Then, the nose twitches! The ears are up! The eyes are staring! You have been seen, and that one suddenly runs from the group!*

*You take him or her in your arms and embrace. Your face is kissed again and again and again, and you look once more into the eyes of your trusting pet.*

*Then, together, you cross the Rainbow Bridge, never again to be separated.*

*—Anonymous*

# CHAPTER 5

## *Cheyanne, The Miracle Dog*

*"If a dog jumps in your lap, it is because he is fond of you; but
if a cat does the same thing, it is because your lap is warmer."*
—*Alfred North Whitehead*

Cheyanne is a cute red-haired beauty I found at the animal shelter. Cheyanne was in the top row, left cage and looked at me with her beautiful brown eyes and I could tell she was the dog for Patches and me. At that time Cheyanne was two years old.

Patches and Cheyanne instantly became friends. Patches went with me to the animal shelter and I slowly introduced her to Cheyanne. Soon they became inseparable and would eat, sleep, and play at the same time. They both loved to take cat naps or should I say cat and dog naps on my bed. They would have slumber parties and lie next to each other and sleep. After their nap they would go and fill their tummies with food and drink before going to play.

After the death of CoCo my mother received a new Siberian Husky puppy from my sister and named him Apache. We had the Spice Girls, CoCo and Ginger, and now it was time for a new beginning . . . Apache and Cheyanne, to honor these two great Indian tribes. Cheyanne and Apache became fast friends. They love to run and play in my mother's large fenced in back yard. When Cheyanne was not with Patches she was with her husband Apache. Cheyanne and Apache get along so well that we tell everyone they are married! When I took Patches to my mother's house to meet Apache, he fell in love with Patches too. I cautiously introduced the big dog to the little cat and it was love at first sight. So when they were all together, Cheyanne, Patches, and Apache would eat, sleep, and play together.

One icy February day, Cheyanne fell on a patch of ice and hit a fence. She became paralyzed from the waist down. Cheyanne loved to run and play outside in the back yard. She would run from one side of the yard to the other. That February there was very much ice from all the snow and rain we had that winter. Cheyanne slid and hit the fence and could not get up. I carried Cheyanne to my car and rushed her to the veterinary office.

The veterinarian immediately took Cheyanne. He pulled on all her legs and stuck needles in her paws. She had no reaction. I was filled with fear and sorrow. Then the dreaded news came. Cheyanne was paralyzed from a spinal cord injury. The veterinarian said it would be a long road if Cheyanne was to recover at all and he could not promise she would improve. I was to give her patience and tender loving care.

At first Cheyanne was very depressed and did not want to eat or drink. She nestled herself in the corner of the living room and did not move for two days. Then on the third day she started to eat and drink for me and her two front legs started to work. Cheyanne would drag her back legs around. Holding Cheyanne in my arms I would pray to do the right thing. She would look up at me lovingly and lick my face and I knew she did not want to give up. Cheyanne knew she was surround by love and support from Apache and Patches too. Apache and Patches would sit and lie by Cheyanne's side giving her love and comfort.

After several long months of prayers, veterinary visits, chiropractor visits, water therapy, and even acupuncture Cheyanne slowly started improving. I bought her a doggie wheel cart, similar to a wheel chair. Her back legs rest on a bar so she can run on her two front legs. Cheyanne ran all around the yard in her doggie wheel cart. My neighbors call Cheyanne the roller queen pup.

One day another dog walked by the house and Cheyanne started to wag her limp tail. I was so happy and amazed. It was about three months after her accident. With each day I could see improvement. Then after about six months she could stand up on her own. I would stand Cheyanne up on her legs and she would stay up for a while. As Cheyanne grew stronger she slowly would take small steps.

With prayers and support from my family and friends Cheyanne grew stronger each day. My dear friend, Mike, gave me a wonderful gift—a tee shirt that says "Animal Rescue" on the back side of the tee shirt and on the front side of the tee shirt is a large photo of Cheyanne. I cherish this tee shirt and love wearing it. Cheyanne even seems to recognize her photo!

They say when you send prayers up to heaven; you receive blessings down on Earth. I know this to be true for after about one year Cheyanne not only walked but also even started running. She still is awkward when she walks and runs but I am so happy. Cheyanne is my wonder dog, or as my veterinarian calls her, Cheyanne, the Miracle Dog!

# CHAPTER 6

## *Birds On A Fence*

*"Life seems to go on without effort,*
*when I am filled with music."*
—*George Eliot*

The summer after Cheyanne's miraculous recovery my neighbor was going on vacation and asked me to watch her parakeet for her. I agreed but was nervous how Patches would react to a parakeet in the house. I reminisced about Sam Wong, #1 Son and Ringo remembering my mother losing her precious antiques.

To protect the parakeet from harm I kept her up on the highest ledge in the house while taking care of her. The parakeet's name was Tweety and I soon found out why that was her name. She tweeted all day long. It was so sweet to hear the little parakeet sing all day long. Patches could hear the singing and just had to investigate. I kept a close eye on Tweety while Patches gazed upon her. Patches's eyes grew bigger and bigger and so did Cheyanne's eyes while watching Tweety and listening to her beautiful singing. Cheyanne and Patches loved gazing upon Tweety listening to her soft music. Both cat and dog spent the entire day just mesmerized by the singing bird.

I was so relieved that Patches did not try to climb up and get Tweety. She was just happy watching the parakeet from afar.

My neighbor was gone for three weeks and we all became very attached to Tweety. When my neighbor came back from vacation and took her little bird back home the house was so quite and Cheyanne and Patches would sadly gaze up where the little sweet tweets had came from.

One day I saw my neighbor outside and mentioned how much Cheyanne and Patches had enjoyed the little bird. Much to my surprise a few days later she presented me with my own parakeet as a thank you for watching her Tweety while she was gone.

Our new parakeet was white and so beautiful. I decided to name him Angel. He filled the house with beautiful music and Patches and Cheyanne seemed so happy. It has been said that when Angels sing their songs are so beautiful and lovely that they spill from heaven to fill every animal, every blade of grass, every flower and tree, every stream and ocean, every rock, stone, and grain of sand with sacred grace. My sweet Angel must have filled the house with beautiful music from the Angels.

I was so afraid that Angel would get lonely so a few days after his arrival I bought another parakeet. He is a beautiful shade of blue similar to the ocean so I named him Aqua. Angel and Aqua are great friends and make beautiful music together.

My mother has a statue of Saint Francis of Assisi in her flowerbed. Whenever I hear Angel and Aqua sing it reminds me of the love Saint Francis of Assisi had for nature and birds. Immense love for everything in the universe so consumed Saint Francis of Assisi that he refused to have a full tonsure shaved into his head so that bugs and vermin, his "more simple brethren," might still have a home in his hair. He considered all animals as his brother or sister. It is said that birds became quiet when he preached and that when he walked through their flocks, they never moved unless he asked it of them. A great poet, Saint Francis himself wrote the following universal prayer.

> *"Lord, make me an instrument of your peace.*
> *Where there is hatred, let me sow love;*
> *Where there is injury, pardon;*
> *Where there is doubt, faith;*
> *Where there is despair, hope;*
> *Where there is darkness, light;*
> *And where there is sadness joy."*

This prayer is especially special to me because it was on my father's prayer cards at his funeral. My father, being the animal lover he was, had a special devotion to St. Francis of Assisi.

Because of the mystical way St. Francis experienced the world, in full possession of and living in divine light, he is invoked to change our view of the world and fill our lives with grace.

Every morning I think of my father and St. Francis of Assisi while attending to Angel and Aqua. Each day after cleaning their cages and giving them fresh water and seeds I throw their previous days seeds out the back door for the wild birds in my yard. After several days of throwing the old seeds outside I started noticing some birds were sitting on my picket fence that goes from my front yard to my back yard. You can see the fence from the living room window and Angel and Aqua started noticing the birds too. Each day the number of birds increased. Soon there were birds lining the fence from the front yard to the back yard. It reminded me of the Alfred Hitchock movie, "***The Birds***" but these were nice birds.

Soon Angel and Aqua were serenading the wild birds and the wild birds sang back in return. Often Patches and Cheyanne would join in the choir also. They would meow and howl along side with all the birds and join in the orchestra too.

When cats and dogs wail and howl it often reminds me of *waits*. *Waits* were a wandering group of singers. In Merrie Olde England, music was an important part of everyday life. Minstrels carried the news of the day from town to town and were often handsomely rewarded for their efforts. In many towns, the *waits* played the role of town criers, singing the hours of the day and reporting local happenings. I think that when you hear a group of birds, cats, or dogs exchanging tweets, meows, and barks they are really catching up on the latest news. Or as William Shakespeare said, "The earth has music for those who listen."

# CHAPTER 7

## *The Too Lovable Cat*

*"Cats do not go for a walk to get somewhere but to explore."*
*—Sidney Denham*

Patches was such a sweet cat. She lived to be 15 years old and died peacefully in her sleep. As Patches grew older and started to eat less and less, Cheyanne seem to watch over Patches and protect her. Cheyanne followed Patches around and would always check on her. When Patches died Cheyanne and I mourned her death deeply. We had lost apart of our family. When Patches had passed away I though about how she had watched over Ginger when she had died and now the favor was returned with Cheyanne watching over Patches. Love is a circle that never ends.

Two months after Patches's death my friend, Alicia, was shopping at a pet store for cat food for her two darling cats, Tori and Chessie. At this pet store there were cats from the Humane Society up for adoption. While walking past the cages glancing at the cats Alicia noticed a cat hiding in his bed. This cat was covered up hiding inside a pocket-like bed. All you could see of this cat were four white paws sticking out of the cave-like bed. Alicia noticed how cute the four white paws were with the soft pink pads. The clerk working at the pet store remarked that the cat was extremely shy. The cat only came out of his cozy cave at night to eat and use the litter box after everyone had gone home. The cat would spend the entire day hiding in his little protective pocket bed. Alicia called me and told me about the cute, shy cat and I just had to go and see this hide-away cat. Once at the pet store I noticed how darling his paws stuck out of his cave-like bed.

I asked the clerk working if I may see the shy cat. Agreeing but warning me of his severe shyness she opened his cage and let me sit on the floor at the opening of the cage door. After a few minutes of speaking softly to the reclusive cat, he lifted up his head and peeked out from his safe hide-away. Cautiously he stood up and crept toward me and I gently started to pet him. Soon he was rubbing up against me and sat on my lap. He purred and purred sitting on my lap as I sweetly stroked him. He was a real beauty—all white with aqua eyes.

I just could not believe that this wonderful cat was up for adoption. He just sat on my lap and while his purring rumbled louder and louder the next thing I knew an hour had passed by. His sweetness and beauty mesmerized me. Holding the cat, scenarios went through my head . . . was this a lost cat? Did someone move and have to get rid of this wonderful cat? Did the cat's previous owner die? It was unbelievable that someone would get rid of this precious cat.

The clerk working at the pet shop smiled at me and said that I had made a friend. I inquired about this sweet cat wondering how it had ended up there for adoption. She stated that the cat had been adopted twice and returned twice. I was filled with such curiosity. "What is the reason the cat was returned?" I asked. The clerk smiled at me and answered, "He is too lovable."

I laughed and laughed and then she laughed and laughed. After brushing the tears away from my laughter. I told the clerk that I would like to adopt this too lovable cat. The third time will be a charm I told her.

I discovered the cat had been named Tucker. I liked that name and decided to officially name him Tucker, the too lovable cat!

# CHAPTER 8

## *Taco Bell*

*"There's no need for a piece of sculpture*
*in a home that has a cat."*
*—Wesley Bates*

After getting Tucker home I was so curious to watch this too lovable cat. I wanted to see this love machine in action.

Tucker seemed just like an average cat. Usually I slowly introduce new pets to their new environment. So I placed Tucker in the bathroom and decided to slowly aquatint him with Cheyanne. But when I cautiously opened the door to leave the bathroom to get Tucker some food he quickly darted out. Spying Cheyanne, Tucker gingerly walked up to her. Cheyanne looked at Tucker and smelled him and then just went and lied down in her bed. Cheyanne must have sensed Tucker's too lovable nature.

With introductions completed, Tucker investigated every nook and cranny of the house. Then Tucker found a warm and cozy spot in front of the window. The sun was coming through the window and glistened on his white fur. Along with being the too lovable cat I soon noticed that he was also the too adorable cat.

In the evening when I sat down to watch some television, Tucker jumped up on my lap and settled down and purred and purred. As the evening went on you could hear his booming purr louder and louder echoing in the room.

When I went to sleep that night Tucker jumped up on my bed. He curled up and went to sleep next to me. During the night he laid himself across my chest and I could hear his thunderous purr. Then later that evening he curled up by my head and buried his face into my hair.

After awakening in the morning I laid in bed thinking about Tucker. I decided that if being too lovable means sleeping on my chest and purring and purring then that's just fine with me. And if being too lovable means sleeping in my hair and gently nuzzling my face, then that's just fine with me too. And if being too lovable means curling up on my lap and purring and purring, then that's just fine with me also. It was settled then, a too lovable cat was just perfect for me.

Later that day I invited my mother over to meet Tucker. He was stretched out on my bed sleeping with the sun's rays glistening across his sparkling white fur when she arrived. I called Tucker's name and when I sweetly called out "Tuucckkeerr," my mother thought that I was calling out, "Taaccoo" instead. Tucker came running over to me. He had a little bell on his collar that was tinkling. When my mother heard his bell jingling and thinking that I had called out, Taaccoo," as he ran toward us, she exclaimed, "Oh, his name is Taco Bell how cute!" So now my too lovable cat had a nickname, Taco Bell!

Sometimes when it is Tucker's dinnertime I will call out, "Taaccoo Belll" and he comes running to get some food. As time went on I noticed that when starting to call out, "Taacco Belll" I would just get out the, "Taa" and here came running Tucker for his food. When Tucker eats his cat food sometimes it starts to slide out of his dish. If I gently turned the dish around while chanting "Taa Taa Taa Taa" then he can eat all the food before it slips out of the dish.

Soon I started noticing that whenever I called out, "Taa Taa Taa Taa" Tucker would come running to me wherever he was.

There is a big pillow on my bed and Tucker likes to lie on it and look outside the window. Sometimes when I wake up in the morning Tucker is lying on the big pillow and staring at me waiting for me to wake up. When I awake and see him eloquently watching me I sleepily say, "Taa Taa Taa Taa" and he jumps up on my chest and purrs and purrs with delight. What a wonderful way to greet a new day.

Who else but a too lovable cat wouldn't mind such a silly nickname as, TaaTaaTaaTaa!

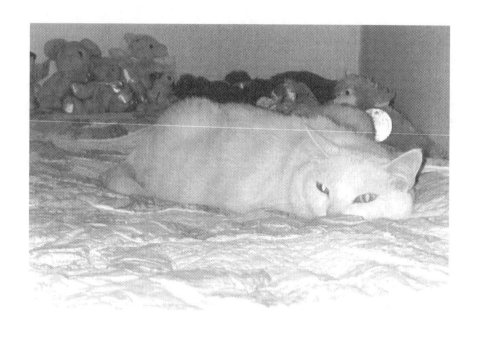

# CHAPTER 9

## *"X Files" Cat*

*"I have studied many philosophers and many cats.
The wisdom of cats is infinitely superior."*
—Hippolyte Taine

I was so excited to have this too lovable cat that I could not wait to tell all my friends about him. Several of my friends are cat experts and asked me if Tucker was deaf. Every time I called out, "Tuucckkeerr," "Taaccoo Bellll," or "TaaTaaTaaTaa" Tucker would come running to me so I knew he was not deaf. My friends explained that many times white cats with blue eyes are deaf.

Doing some research, I found out that dominant white cats with blue eyes have an increased chance of becoming deaf. Cats with one blue eye have a big chance to become deaf on the blue-eye side. Cats with orange eyes will probably be less deaf. Some dominant white kittens are born with a tuft of colored hair on top of the head, this usually disappears when they grow older, but these kittens have a better chance of normal hearing.

Further research revealed that there is a connection between the white fur color, blue eyes and deafness. Deafness is linked to the gene for blue eyes and not to the gene for dissimilar eyes. It depends on the cat's genetic structure and not on the cat's appearance. One of the genes for the development of white fur both influences the eyes and the ears. This gene can cause a lack of eye pigmentation in blue eyes and can cause deafness. Since the eyes and ears can be found close to each other the gene which influences that part of the body will probably influence both senses. So, in general blue-eye white cats have a larger chance to become deaf than other cats, but it isn't guaranteed that they are deaf.

I was so happy that my Tucker was not deaf and could hear me. One day while watching an episode of the 'X Files' I whistled along with the 'X Files' theme music of the show. Tucker came running to me and listened while I was whistling. He seemed to love the sound of the 'X Files' whistle. The next day another episode came on and the same thing happened, as I whistled Tucker came running. Sometimes throughout the day I would just whistle the 'X Files' tune randomly and here came Tucker. Whenever I wanted Tucker I just whistled the 'X Files' tune. It was so adorable. He always came running. Since then I have come to notice he also likes me to whistle the theme music to 'Last of the Summer Wine', a British comedy. I whistle the 'Last of the Summer Wine' theme music when it is brushing time and when it is petting time I whistle the 'X Files' tune. Even Cheyanne recognizes the whistles and comes running too!

# Chapter 10

## *"Hello Tucker"*

*"The ideal of calm exists in a sitting cat."*
*—Jules Reynard*

My friend, Alicia, who found Tucker for me, has the cutest voice mail. If you push the number 1 on the key pad you get to speak to Alicia's husband, if you push number 2 you get to speak to Alicia, but if you push number 3 you get to talk to her two cats, Chessie and Tori. After you push the number 3 on the phone pad you can hear an adorable "Meow" from Chessie and Tori. I always push number 3 when leaving Alicia a message just so I can hear the adorable "Meow."

Soon cat messages were arriving for Tucker, the too lovable cat, too!

One day I came home from work late and noticed there were several messages on my answering machine. The first message was from my mother. We always talk on the phone when I get home from work and catch up on daily events. After mom realized I wasn't home she decided to leave Tucker a message. It went something like this, "Taaccoo Belll is your mommy still at work? Are you being a good boy? Tell your mommy I will call her back later." When I heard this message I smiled to myself thinking how cute it was.

Then I listened to the next message and it was from my sister. Soon I realized the same thing happened. When my sister realized I was not at home she left a message for Tucker too. She said, "Tucker is your mommy still at work? Are you keeping an eye on the house until mommy gets back? Are you watching those birds? Is your mouth drooling? Well, tell your mommy I will call back soon." I laughed as the next message from my boyfriend came on. After he realized I was not home from work yet he did the same thing. "Tucker where is that Anna Bananna? Is she still at work? Meeeoweeee. Meeeoweee." Then he whistled the 'X Files' tune. I laughed and laughed after hearing all those messages.

Soon I was to come home from outings and find only messages for Tucker. Each time my mother would call me the message would start out, "Well, Hello Taaccoo Belll."

One day my sister left an unusual message: "Tucker, here is today's headlines: **Man devastated; woman leaves man for cat!** Tell mommy to call me when she gets home." After calling my sister back I found out she broke up with her boyfriend and wanted Tucker to be her new boyfriend!

Tucker, the too lovable cat, still comes running when I whistle the 'Last of the Summer Wine' theme song and the 'X Files' tune. But now he also comes running to the phone when he gets messages. Tucker sure is a busy cat with all these messages coming in. It is a blessing that he is not deaf as some blue-eyed, white cats. How else could he hear all these cute messages!

# CHAPTER 11

## Flip-Flop, the Miracle Goldfish

*"Look twice before you leap."*
*—Charlotte Bronte'*

Cheyanne and Tucker became fast friends. I was so worried about how this too lovable cat would react to the parakeets and my 7 year-old goldfish, Flip-Flop. Would Tucker be too lovable with them or would he look upon them as prey? But Tucker's too lovable side is just too lovable and he just gazes upon the birds and the goldfish and never tries to get them. Patches was so subdued that she never bothered them either.

One day my goldfish, Flip-Flop became sick because his water became too cold after a power outage. It took several days for him to recover. Cheyanne and Tucker would look up at his fish tank sensing Flip-Flop was sick. It was as if they were watching over him until he recovered. What other goldfish has a miracle dog and a too lovable cat that watches over him. Not to mention, Angel and Aqua. They just love to watch Flip-Flop swim around in his fish tank.

One day I was cleaning out Flip-Flop's tank and thought it would be a good idea to make his tank higher on the table so he could see his reflection in the big mirror on the wall. I found a board that was just the perfect height to put under Flip-Flop's tank, but it stuck out about one-foot longer than the table. After realizing the board was too long and deciding to remove it, I noticed it was almost time for me to go to work. So I decided to finish moving the board later after returning home from work.

While I was at work, Tucker, the too lovable cat, wanted a better look at Flip-Flop. Tucker jumped up on the board and Flip-Flop's tank turned upside down. When I came home from work and looked in the living room I saw the fish tank upside down and all the water on the floor. I frantically searched for Flip-Flop expecting the worse.

All of a sudden I glanced over at Tucker and noticed he was sitting looking into the bucket that I had been using to clean out Flip-Flop's tank. I ran over and looked into the bucket and there was Flip-Flop swimming around in the bucket in only about one-inch of water. Tucker was patiently waiting for me to notice Flip-Flop. I could not believe my eyes and was so happy that my dear Flip-Flop was all right. Tucker, the too lovable cat, watched over Flip-Flop until my return home.

After this incident I affectionately called Flip-Flop, the miracle goldfish. If I have a too lovable cat and a miracle dog why couldn't I have a miracle goldfish too!

# CHAPTER 12

## *Ginny Gonzalez*

*"Cats sleep fat and walk thin."*
—*Rosalie Moore*

There are miracles around us everywhere. Cheyanne, is the miracle dog and Flip-Flop is the miracle goldfish. There was another miracle dog besides Cheyanne named Ginny Gonzalez. Her story is remarkable. Ginny was the Mother Teresa of cats. Here is her story.

Philip Gonzalez who lives in New York had lost interest in life after an industrial accident left him disabled. His best friend, Sheilah Harris, persuaded Philip to adopt a dog. He found a badly abused one-year-old dog with soft brown eyes and a cute grin at a local animal shelter. This was an abused dog who had been abandoned, locked in a closet when her drug addict owner moved out and left Ginny to starve and die along with her three puppies. The animal shelter brought Ginny and her three puppies back to life and put them up for adoption.

At first Philip had reservations about adopting a dog but after spending time with the dog he adopted her. Sheilah collects Ginny dolls, similar to Barbie dolls, and so in honor of his friend Philip named the little mixed dog, Ginny.

Soon Philip realized that Ginny was no ordinary dog. Whimpering and pulling on her leash, she dragged Philip into a vacant lot on their first walk together. Ginny found a starving stray cat and coerces Philip into feeding the helpless cat. A month later, after finding and feeding dozens of stray cats, Philip and Ginny went back to the animal shelter to get Ginny her own cat. From a roomful of playful kittens, Ginny chooses the one kitten that would turn out to be completely deaf. But one handicapped cat was not enough for Ginny. Soon her amazing radar of the heart led her to rescue a cat with only one eye, a cat with no hind feet, and a paralyzed kitten whom Ginny found abandoned in an empty building.

Ginny was the Mother Teresa of sick and disabled cats. Ginny had a loving sixth sense radar, and could pick out sick and injured animals from bushes, from buildings, from trailers, brown paper bags, from empty boxes, cartons of broken glass, garbage cans, air-conditioning ducts, eight-inch pipes, and other unlikely places.

While walking past a gas station Ginny ran up on a pickup truck parked nearby that belonged to a landscaping company; its open truck bed was filled with sod and heavy grass clippings. The cab was empty; the driver was probably at lunch not knowing a small cat was trapped. Ginny ran to it, jumped right up into the truck, and began digging through the packed sod. Ginny dug down to where a small cat was pinned under the sod and unable to move. Rushing over to Ginny, Philip set the soon smothered cat free. As soon as she was out of danger, she began to purr at the top of her lungs.

One night while walking Ginny she dashed away and ran to a fence where a helpless cat was caught on barbed wire, hanging unable to get down. The terrified cat was struggling desperately and the barbed wire was cutting into her. Ginny put her paws up on the fence and whimpered straight at the cat, as though talking to her, and the cat heard her, stopped its struggling, braced itself, gave a sudden leap and tore itself free landing at Ginny. The cat rubbed against Ginny affectionately as though saying, "thanks for saving me."

One day while walking Ginny past a glass company Ginny ran off and began digging furiously in a carton overflowing with broken glass. She kept on pawing through the knifelike shards with all her energy. By the time Philip reached Ginny she had bloody paws and was limping, dangling a bloody, near-death kitten from her jaw. Ginny's paws and the kitten were covered with splinters of glass. Both kitten and Ginny recovered and became inseparable.

Ginny made it clear that as long as there was an abused cat, an injured cat, a disabled cat, a disfigured cat, a cat in trouble or in pain, she would find it with her special radar and compel Philip to help her.

As long as there was a cat out there who needed an extra helping of love and understanding, Ginny was not far behind. Ginny was a living lesson in fur, a lesson that kindness and caring work miracles.

Ginny's innate sixth sense for rescuing cats and her angelic mission gave Philip a new sense of purpose and a new lease on life. Or as Philip has stated, "I really do believe that Ginny was an angel, sent down to do specific rescue work. When you consider how many lives she saved and made better—starting with my own—you can see that she had to be on a mission from heaven. I believe that God sent Ginny down to rescue me. In my old life, I had plenty of fun, but no real happiness. Now I know the true happiness of living for others, and the true happiness of being surrounded by creatures I love.

Most of all, little Ginny—part Schnauzer, part Siberian Husky, part angel from heaven—taught me the most important lesson in life. Life is not worth living without love, that giving love is more rewarding than getting it, and that the humblest creatures, the least advantaged creatures, are worthy of the greatest outpouring of love. It's a spiritual message, that all life is precious, all life is short, and that, just as human beings have immortal souls, so do animals have immortal souls, because they, too, were created by God."

> *"There's a group I'm almost looking forward to reuniting*
> *with on The Other Side more than all the others put*
> *together—every pet we've ever had, from every lifetime*
> *we've experienced, gathers around us with such urgent joy*
> *that the people waiting to welcome us have a hard time*
> *getting to us through the happy crowd of animals."*

> —*Sylvia Browne*

# CHAPTER 13

## *Blessing of the Animals*

*"Animals are such agreeable friends—they ask*
*no questions, they pass no criticisms."*
*—George Eliot*

The animals have a special day known as the Blessing of the Animals Ceremony. Creatures great and small crowd churches all across America, as these places of worship throw open their doors. Most churches celebrate this day on October 4th, the feast day of St. Francis of Assisi, who was named patron saint of ecology by John Paul II in 1979. Though St. Anthony the Abbot and others can also be named as patron saints of animals, the ceremony most often is associated with St. Francis. His love and respect for animals has forever linked St. Francis of Assisi with the Blessing of the Animals Ceremony through his words: "Creatures minister to our needs every day. Without them we could not live, and through them the human race greatly offends the Creator every time we fail to appreciate so great a blessing."

There is some visual evidence depicting early animal blessings, drawings in medieval manuscripts showing St. Anthony the Abbot performing an animal blessing. Formal church organized animal blessings were held in Rome in the early 20th century, while in the United States, the Catholic Church began blessing animals in honor of St. Anthony the Abbot in the historic Olvera Street area of downtown Los Angeles in the 1930s.

On the East Coast, another Blessing of the Animals Ceremony is held annually at the Episcopal Cathedral of New York's St. John the Divine. Thousands of people, along with animals pack into the world's largest

Gothic cathedral for a joyous and solemn religious service that celebrates all living things. The procession has included elephants, camels, oxen, horses, ferrets, and a golden eagle.

At the Basilica of St. Mary in Minneapolis a yak walked down the center aisle of the church during the parade of animals.

All across America churches celebrate this unique blessings of the animals. This ceremony is intended to reconnect people with the importance of animals in their lives and in God's plan of creation and recognizing and celebrating the remarkable creative love that God has bestowed on the world, and honoring how God touches us through each of his creatures.

St. Anthony the Abbot was also known as St. Anthony the Great and St. Anthony of Egypt. This desert father and patron of the animal kingdom spent his early adulthood helping to care for his younger sister after his parents' deaths. When his sister was grown, he sold all he had and gave the money to the poor. St. Anthony then headed for the desert. He lived alone for many years, but as word of his holiness spread, the number of visitors increased. He founded two monasteries, and was thought to be a great healer. One story tells of the many animals St. Anthony encountered during his travels—including a wolf that led him to St. Paul, a raven that brought them food, and later, a lion that helped to dig St. Paul's grave.

St. Albert the Great Catholic Church in Dayton, Ohio has a Blessing of the Animals Ceremony. All kinds of cute furry creatures can be found that day being blessed. When the priest blesses the animals out in front of the church even the wild outdoor animals get a blessing. There are squirrels running around in the trees on the grounds watching the ceremony down below. One can just feel that the squirrels understand the meaning of the ceremony and rejoice along with all the pets below.

One day my neighbor, Andy, and I found a baby squirrel lying on the ground. It was so tiny that we were not sure what it was. We thought maybe that it was a baby possum, mole, or raccoon. After some research Andy found out it was a baby squirrel that had fallen out of the nest that was high up in the tree. He rode his bike many miles away to a pet store and bought all kinds of supplies to nurse the baby squirrel back to health. The little squirrel lived for a few days. It was sad when the little baby squirrel died and I respected Andy for his efforts. Whenever I see cute squirrels running around I think about that baby squirrel and how it touched our hearts.

A few years later another baby squirrel would enter my life. There was a scratching sound coming from the walls of my house. At first I kept thinking it was mice in the walls but the sounds were louder and louder. After a few days the sounds were accompanied by chirp sounds and squeaks. I determined that the squeaks and chirps were not from mice and I wondered what was in the wall. I knew it must be an animal that was stuck in the wall so I took a hammer and gently made a small hole then I picked at the hole until it was bigger and bigger. I saw the baby squirrel's paws clawing along with mine. At first I was scared because I was not sure what to do once the squirrel came out of the wall, but I found my parakeets smaller cage that had been replaced by a bigger cage. I opened the cage door and put the cage in front of the hole and watched as the squirrel made the hole big enough to get out of the wall and then he ran into the cage. I quickly closed the door of the cage and took the squirrel outside.

Once outside I opened the cage door and the little squirrel scurried out and was so happy to be released. I felt so sorry for the little squirrel because his tail was crooked from being stuck in the wall and he was walking a little funny too. But as I watched the squirrel he shook his tail and it straighten out and he leaped up a tree and joyfully reunited with other squirrels.

As I contemplate the squirrels and the Blessing of the Animals Ceremony I realize how blessed I am to have such sweet dear pets in my life. It makes one realize that the most important gifts in life are love, kindness, and joy and it's not the things we get but the hearts we touch that will determine the richness of our life. My heart has been touched and my life has been blessed with all these gifts from having animals in my life, especially a too lovable cat named, Tucker.

*"If all the beasts were gone, men would die from a great loneliness of spirit, for whatever happens to the beasts also happens to the man. All things are connected."*

*—Chief Seattle of the Suwamish tribe, letter to U.S. President Franklin Pierce (mid 1800s)*

# CHAPTER 14

## *Serendipity and a Cat Named Emerald*

*"In a cat's eye, all things belong to cats."*
*—English proverb*

**Serendipity** is the effect by which one accidentally discovers something fortunate, especially while looking for something else entirely.

Some scientists and inventors are reluctant about reporting accidental discoveries, others openly admit its role; in fact serendipity is a major component of scientific discoveries and inventions.

Serendipity is defined as a knack of stumbling upon interesting discoveries in a casual manner. Like when Ivory Soap was invented. Ivory Soap was invented by accident when an employee at the Proctor and Gamble Company, in Cincinnati, accidentally left a batch of soap mixing for too long. Even though air had been worked into the mixture, the soap was poured into bars and sold. Soon many people were writing the company asking for more bars of the "soap that floats." Harley Proctor, of Proctor and Gamble, was inspired to name the soap Ivory when he read the words "out of ivory palaces" in the Bible at church one Sunday morning in 1879.

Other discoveries accidentally invented are: Teflon, Super-glue, Scotchgard, Cellophane, Penicillin, Smallpox vaccine, Discovery of the planet Uranus, WD-40, the Microwave oven, X-ray machine, Corn Flakes and Wheaties, and Post-It Notes.

I believe that serendipity, coincidences, and miracles are all examples of our guardian angels at work.

When Cheyanne had her accident one coincidence led to another resulting in a miracle. It was not just a coincidence that my friend just happened to mention that her Chiropractor worked on dogs. Then another friend mentioned to me that Acupuncture had amazing healing qualities and then I found an Acupuncturist that worked on dogs.

I was not looking for a new cat when Alicia told me about Tucker. This sweet cat, that is too lovable, has blessed my life with such love.

Serendipity was to enter my life once again on a cold Easter day. I went to a dear friend's house to drop off an Easter basket and wish her Easter blessings. Mary Lu was not at home that day but I discovered a little, terribly thin, black cat sitting at her front door. Glancing down at the cat I thought that maybe Mary Lu had gotten a cat since my last visit of only two weeks ago. But the cat looked so scraggily and thin. After knocking on Mary Lu's door several times and realizing she was not at home I decided to write her a note.

Going back inside my car I sat and was searching in my purse for a piece of paper and a pen. Sitting there it felt as if I was being watched. Glancing over at the passenger's side of the car there was the little black cat staring back at me. He must have dashed into my car while I wasn't looking. After realizing there was no paper or pen in my purse I remember there was some in my trunk. So I got out of the car and the little black cat followed me out.

Going to the trunk of my car I found a piece of paper and a pen in which to write a greeting to Mary Lu. I decided to sit and write my note inside the car. After going back to the front of my car I noticed that the little black cat was still following me. Gingerly opening up the car door so the cat would not get back inside my car I sat down and glanced downward and did not see the cat and quickly closed the car door and started to write my note to Mary Lu. While I was writing my note, the same feeling overwhelmed me—that I was being watched. Looking over at the passenger's seat, low and behold, there was the black cat again! How could he have scurried into my car so fast a second time without me noticing it? After finishing my note and getting out of the car to put the note on Mary Lu's door the cat once again followed me out of the car up to the door. I hung a bag containing my little Easter basket and note on the doorknob of the front door. Sitting down at my feet was the little black cat. I decided to pet the cat and reason with him that he could not go for a ride in my car. While petting the cat I noticed he was pathetically thin and frail. How could he have even had the strength to jump into my car, not let alone once but twice? My heart went out to this tiny black cat.

Walking back to my car I opened the door and saw the little darling jump in and run as fast as he could behind my driver's seat and around to the front passenger seat. Sitting there pretty as you please just looking at me with his beautiful green eyes. I decided then and there that this cat was going home with me. The third times a charm again!

Getting home I opened a can of cat food and the little black cat ate like there was no tomorrow. Then I found a little bed that Tucker never slept in and placed it in front of the little black cat. He walked right into that bed and fell asleep. Whenever a new pet enters an established pet zone it is always a worry how the pets will react to the new addition; but immediately Tucker, the too lovable cat, and Cheyanne, the miracle dog, took a liking to this new family member.

The next day I called Mary Lu and told her about the black cat. She stated that there was a stray black cat in the neighborhood and some of the neighbors were putting food out for the cat. They felt sorry for the poor thing living outside in such cold damp weather. I told Mary Lu about the cat jumping in my car three times and she was amazed, and happy that the cat found a safe warm home.

I decided to name the cat Emerald because his eyes were as green as the Emerald Isle, Ireland. My Irish mother likes that.

It was serendipity when I found Emerald. I was going to my friend's house to drop off a gift and in return I received an adorable black, green-eyed, furry gift instead. Maybe it was serendipity, maybe it was Ginny Gonzalez's spirit or maybe it was the Great Pawnee legend that led me to Emerald.

*"There is a Pawnee legend that states when a person is in need of an animal friend that many times the animal sent is a stricken or helpless*

*creature to encourage the person to care for it. This is why so many people who have taken in stray animals come to feel that the animal they almost did not rescue became the most precious being they know, and that the day they found this dear animal was the luckiest day of their lives."*

I am among one of these lucky people, for the day I met Cheyanne, the miracle dog; Tucker, the too lovable cat; and Emerald, the Serendipity cat changed my life forever.

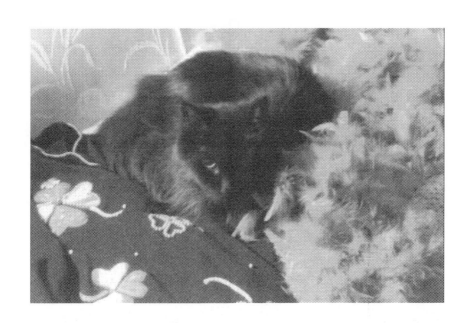

# CHAPTER 15

## *Henrietta, the Cat who Covered the World*

*"Of all God's creatures, there is only one that cannot
be made slave of the leash. That one is the cat. If
man could be crossed with the cat it would improve
the man, but it would deteriorate the cat."*
—*Mark Twain*

Tucker and Emerald and Cheyanne became great friends. We all had a big relocation when my mother became very ill and could not live alone any more. I moved back home to take care of her and Tucker, Emerald, and Cheyanne adjusted to the move very well, not to mention Aqua, Angel, and Flip-Flop.

The previous year I had to stay at a hotel for two months while my house was being renovated from ice damage. My insurance company found a hotel where I could take all my pets with me. It was like taking a vacation. I was worried sick that all my dear pets would wonder what was going on with us moving into a strange place but as long as we were all together they were fine. They looked upon it as a great adventure.

Our big moves reminded me of the wonderful book, <u>The Cat Who Covered The World,</u> by Christopher S. Wren. Christopher Wren gave his two children, Celia and Chris, a tiny kitten one Christmas. The children named the part Siamese cat after Henrietta a puppet on their favorite television show, '***Mister Rogers' Neighborhood'***.

Henrietta was a very special kitty. Originally from New York City. She ventured overseas with foreign correspondent Christopher Wren along with his wife and children. Over seventeen years and tens of thousands of miles, Henrietta became companion for the reporter as he covered world events in Moscow, Cairo, Beijing, Ottawa, and Johannesburg. Not to mention visits to Paris, Rome, Lisbon, and Tokyo.

Our moves were not as awesome as Henrietta's travels around the world but they seemed adventurous just the same. The biggest excitement at the hotel occurred when the fire alarm went off in the middle of the night. I was uncertain whether it was an actual fire or not but I could not leave all my feathered friends behind so I made several trips in and out of the hotel until all pets were safe standing outside with me. It was a real sight. We gathered quite a crowd—forget the fire engines; cats, dog, fish, and birds were more important! Everyone walked over to see all my beloved friends. Licks and pats galore. Tucker strolled along and rubbed up against everyone with his deep loud purring. "Oh, what a beautiful cat, squealed one little girl." "Look at those eyes!" exclaimed another. Yes. Tucker, the too lovable cat, was enjoying all this attention. It was a fun time and we were all relieved to know there was no fire and that it had been a false alarm. When it was all over and we were allowed back into the building the last fire engine drove off and Tucker was still being fussed over. I even had help carrying all my pets back to my room. As I glanced back to see who was carrying Tucker, I saw two women carrying him . . . one holding his two front paws and the other his torso and back paws, stroking him all the while. Tucker was living up to his reputation . . . the too lovable cat.

Cheyanne was becoming a celebrity at the hotel too. Every time someone saw me take Cheyanne outside to do her business they came over to pet her. I told them about her book and the word was spreading. Soon everyone wanted to see Cheyanne, the miracle dog. I even thought they might put my book, Cheyanne, the Miracle Dog on display in the lobby until my dreams were dashed. One evening while I was taking Cheyanne outside just before bedtime to relieve her I did not get her outside in time and she did her business in the lobby right in front of the night clerk. Needless to say I was worried this incident could ruin our reputation but the clerk was busy on the phone and did not seem to notice so I quickly picked up the evidence with my tissue hoping no one was the wiser. Everything seemed fine until about two months later after returning home when I received a bill from the hotel. The bill was for carpet cleaning. The reason—pet soiled in lobby.

# CHAPTER 16

## *Calum Sweeney*

*"Cats are connoisseurs of comfort."*
—*James Herriot*

After I moved back home to help my mother Cheyanne was so happy to be with Apache full-time and Apache liked the company of Cheyanne along with Tucker and Emerald.

One day a box came for my mother. After emptying the box I placed it on the floor. Later I noticed that Emerald had climbed into the box and fell fast asleep. If that sight was not cute enough I noticed that written largely on the side of the box was "FRAGIL Handle with Care." That summed it up in a nutshell, Emerald was fragile and was to be handled with care. Even Apache realized this. Apache seemed to watch over Emerald with a protective nature. He even became a bed partner with Emerald; that is when Emerald was not in his box. Apache and Emerald would cuddle up and take naps together. It has been noted that Siberian Huskies do not like cats but my Apache proves this theory wrong; he liked Patches and loves Tucker and Emerald.

One day a friend stopped by with a gift and forgot to close the door behind him. After a nice visit we noticed a missing Tucker around the house. Tucker always stayed near us and it was so unusual when we did not see him nearby. Then I remembered that the door had been ajar. My friend and I walked around the neighborhood searching for Tucker. We did not find Tucker because he was fast asleep in the empty box my friend's gift came in! Tucker always peeked in at Emerald in his box and I think he wanted his own box!

But serendipity entered our lives again, while searching outside for Tucker we found another cat. He was a dirty, thin cat and it looked like he had not eaten in weeks. We took the cat home and fed him. Tucker jumped out of the box to see what all the commotion was about. I was so relieved to see my Tucker and greeted him lovingly exclaiming, "Oh, there you are! We were searching for you outside and found this kitty instead. Were you hiding from us so we would go out and find this little fellow?" I truly think that Tucker did just that. It was as if Tucker hid in that box so we would go out searching for him, but find this cat that needed our love and attention instead. When we returned home with the stray cat Tucker just jumped out of the box and looked at me as if to say, "I knew you would find him." Tucker hid in that box so we would think he was outside and while searching for him we would find this starving cat. Ginny Gonzalez I am sure had a hand in this matter too.

After giving the stray cat a bath we realized how beautiful he was, and he had the most beautiful sparkling greenish brown eyes. Earlier that day my mother had been reminiscing about her uncle, Calum Sweeney, and how he was a great sprinter. He won many metals and she was showing them to me. I thought that serendipity was once again at work and decided to name the sweet cat we found after my great uncle, Calum Sweeney.

The next day we took Calum Sweeney to the veterinary and found out that the cat was very ill. He had water on his lungs and had a very bad heart. The veterinary told us that he probably would not live long and wanted to know if we wanted to put the cat down, but we decided to keep him.

Calum Sweeney was the most wonderful cat. He joined our family famously and we all became attached to him. He was so kind and gentle. Apache, Cheyanne, Tucker, and Emerald sensed Calum's weakness and were very gentle toward him. Calum graced us with his presence for almost a year before he died peacefully one night. I like to think that we made Calum's last year happy and loving, and that there are two Calum Sweeney's in heaven. One Calum Sweeney holding the other Calum Sweeney, each taking care of the other until that day when we are all reunited.

*"The best and most beautiful things in the world cannot be seen or even touched—they must be felt with the heart."*
*—Helen Keller*

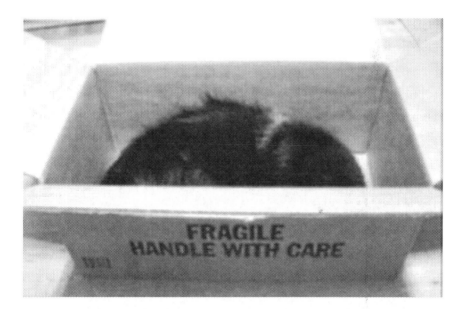

# CHAPTER 17

## *Penny and Zoe*

*"One cat just leads to another."*
*—Ernest Hemingway*

My friends, John and Janice, are great animal lovers. They have saved many stray cats. There was a special little dog they saved from a harsh winter, but more on that later.

Janice and John have hearts of gold. Their love of animals is well known. On Carlisle Street one day, two little boys holding a tiny kitten approached Janice. The two young boys must have sensed Janice's tender heart. The boys asked Janice if she would care for their little kitten because their mother and father would not let them keep any more cats. The boys had one condition for Janice, that she would keep the tiny kitten's name—Penelope. Janice looked at the tiny fur ball and could not refuse.

Janice already had many cats, some stray, she was taking care of and worried about the tiny kitten. She knew how loving Tucker and Emerald were and asked me if I would like Penelope. I thought that Tucker and Emerald might like a new playmate after mourning the death of Calum Sweeney so I agreed. Janice mentioned about the two little boys on Carlisle Street and how they wanted Penelope to keep her name. I thought it would be cute to name the new kitten "Kitty Carlisle" after the 1960's entertainer my mother loved to watch on television. But Penelope it was, and Kitty Carlisle could be her nickname.

Penelope was a very playful kitty and Tucker and Emerald loved to watch Penelope run and play. Tucker and Emerald would join in the fun until they became tired and then they would go off and take a catnap.

When I called out to Penelope it seemed so long and awkward calling out "PENELOPE," especially when she was sliding across a table or trying to jump up on Cheyanne's back. So one day while I hurriedly called out to her before she broke a dish, I shouted, "PENNY" and she looked up at me and stopped dead in her tracks. As time went on and I called her "Penny" more and more she seemed to like the shortened version of "Penelope." Each time I called out "PENNY" she would come running to me. So now our Penelope had two nicknames, Penny and Kitty Carlisle.

Tucker loved Penny so much that he became her surrogate mother. Penny would knead at Tucker's belly and start nursing his nipples. Tucker just lied there for hours and let Penny nurse him. Mind you, Tucker is a male cat, but Penny did not seem to know that or care. Penny did not even seem to mind that milk was not coming out. Who else but the world's most lovable cat would let a tiny kitten nurse him for hours on end?

A few months later, John and Janice were going on vacation and asked me if I could watch a cat for them. The cat's named was Zoe. Zoe was a stray cat that had been living in an alley for years since her owner died and she had no where to go. It took John and Janice years to earn the cats trust. They put food out for the cat everyday until finally one day they were able to pet Zoe.

Zoe is a beautiful white cat with black markings. On one side of Zoe is the shape of a heart. I thought that was a sign because my mother's birthday is on Valentine's Day. Zoe is so delicate and graceful and walks like a ballerina. As the days went by my mother and I grew more and more attached to Zoe. When John and Janice came back from vacation I mentioned how much my mother and I liked Zoe. They asked me if we would consider keeping Zoe. And that is how a white alley cat with a black shaped heart on her fur stole my heart and joined our family of pets.

Zoe is very independent and likes to be on her own. She does not interact too much with our array of cats and dogs. But Zoe just loves my mother.

Every night Zoe sleeps with my mother and cuddles her all day long. It must be serendipity again, how else would a cat with a heart on her fur fall so much in love with a Valentine mommy.

When Zoe is not with my mother she likes to lie on the window ledge and look outside. But lately she has let a too lovable cat share her window ledge and food. Leave it to Tucker to warm the heart of an alley cat.

# CHAPTER 18

## *The Little Dog*

*"Dogs come when they're called; cats take a
message and get back to you later."*
*—Mary Bly*

For months my friends had spoken about the, "Little Dog." There was a
little dog outside all spring and now into late summer. It had been a very
hot summer and they worried about her having enough water to drink
and food to eat. John, Janice, Bob, and Barbara would put food out for the
Little Dog. The Little Dog would gobble the food down and then run off
into the woods again. Even the neighbors across the street were concerned
and started feeding the Little Dog. As summer drew to an end and the
beautiful leaves of autumn fell all were concerned about the Little Dog
and winter drawing near. Every time someone would approach the Little
Dog, it would seem frightened and run off into the woods again.

Then at Christmas time all Bob could think of was the Little Dog. He
had not seen the Little Dog for at least one month. It was already cold
outside and snow was beginning to fall. I tried to reassure him that maybe
someone took the Little Dog in, but he remembered how many times he
had tried to befriend the Little Dog only to get close and have the dog run
off into the woods again.

Bob decided to go to the animal shelter and look for the Little Dog. He
could not believe his luck when he found the Little Dog there. The Little
Dog had been there for six weeks. Bob frantically called me. He was afraid
that the Little Dog had been there for too long and would be put down.
He had to go to work, so I drove over to the animal shelter that cold
January day.

Entering the animal shelter it dawned on me that I was not sure what the Little Dog looked like, as I had never seen her. So I asked the woman working if I could see the Little Dog that Bob had just seen. She replied, "Oh, the Boston Terrier." Then she called back to the kennel and asked the clerk to bring out the Boston Terrier. As I waited in the lobby I thought of the musical "*Annie.*" I thought that Annie's dog, Sandy, was a Boston Terrier. Then I started to think of the song, '*Tomorrow*' that Annie sang. The words were racing through my head as a clerk entered the lobby and stood near me with a little dog.

Mind you, I did not realize that this little dog was our 'Little Dog'. I thought the clerk was exercising the little dog around the lobby. The little dog walked around the lobby for a while then came over to me and I petted her and told the clerk what a cute dog she was. The little dog sat down at my feet and just gazed upon me. At first glance I thought the little dog looked like a miniature bulldog. Then I remembered that my parent's previous neighbors, Claudina and Jim, had a doggie that looked just like that. Her name was Mitzy and she was the sweetest doggie. This little dog also had a flat pug nose and she was snorting just like Mitzy had. As I stood there thinking about Claudina, Jim, and Mitzy I wondered where the Boston Terrier was that I was sure would look like the dog, Sandy, from the musical "*Annie.*" Later I was to find out that Sandy was an indistinguishable breed of dog, which was also found at an animal shelter.

After a few minutes two more clerks walked into the lobby from the back room where all the dogs were kept. I asked them if they could go back and bring out the Boston Terrier. The two clerks looked at me then glanced at each other, then gazed upon the little dog at my feet. Then they looked at the clerk who originally brought out the little dog and then glanced at each other again before finally looking at me and pointed to the little dog saying, "That is the only Boston Terrier we have." I felt so silly. I explained to them that I did not know what a Boston Terrier looked like, but I did not realize that it looked like this. Laughter abound, even the Little Dog seemed to grin.

Later after Barbara, Bob, Janice, and John returned to the animal shelter, my friends adopted a new little dog that day. Their house was already over ran with many pets, some ill so I took the Little Dog home with me. Cheyanne and Apache could have a new little companion. Little Dog did not seem to do her justice, so I renamed her Eva. One of my mother's friends, a doggie lover, is Eva and I have always loved that name.

My Eva may not be a Broadway star like Sandy from the musical *"Annie"*, but she is a star just the same to me. She is very loving and a sweet little dog. Her nickname is Eva Las Vegas. She ran in circles one day when Elvis was on television singing '*Viva Las Vegas*', so I nicknamed her Eva Las Vegas! Maybe Eva is a Broadway star after all!

When I took Eva to the veterinary office for the first time the veterinary assistant, Carol, was excited to meet Eva. She remarked that she had a Boston Terrier that looked just like Eva when she was growing up. One winter there was a very bad snowstorm and her dog went outside and became stuck in a big snowdrift. It took several days before they found the little dog and then they had to dig her out. Carol mentioned how resilient and intelligent Boston Terriers are. How else could her dog have lasted so long in that terrible snowdrift.

Julie Klam has written a wonderful book about her life with Boston Terriers entitled, You Had Me At Woof. Klam has worked with the Northeast Boston Terrier Rescue. In her book, Klam states; "I found out that the Boston terrier originated when an English bulldog and an English terrier were bred and then the product was bred with a bulldog. Though they were not intentionally bred for it, Boston Terriers have a very pronounced loyalty to their masters. Because they looked like they are formally dressed wearing tuxedos, they were nicknamed the 'American Gentleman'." After reading this, I glanced down at Eva and noticed that it did look like she is wearing a tuxedo. Eva even looks like she is wearing elegant white boots. She was looking quite dapper! The more that I thought about it, maybe Eva should be on Broadway. I could just see her on the stage in her little tuxedo and boots dancing to '*Viva Las Vegas*'.

Tucker fell in love with Eva at first sight. Tucker shares his food with Eva and even his bed. Eva lets Tucker sample her food first and then when Tucker is full Eva finishes up the dish. They even share the same bed. Tucker loves to snuggle up and sleep with Eva. The only problem is that sometimes Eva snores so loud it wakes up Tucker. Then Tucker goes off and explores while Eva finishes up her nap.

It only makes since that the too lovable cat would fall in love with a little dog that snorts and snores. Little Eva has snorted and snored her way into our hearts.

# CHAPTER 19

## *Tucker, Super Hero*

*"If we treated everyone we meet with the same affection*
*we bestow upon our favorite cat, they too, would purr."*
—Martin Buxbaum

Tucker's lovable nature was being well know to all my family and friends. Soon I started to notice that friends would come over and ask the whereabouts of Tucker. If I replied that he was taking a catnap on my bed. They would look on my bed and squeal out, "Oh, how adorable!" Yes, Tucker's lovable status was growing each day. As time went on Tucker's popularity and heroics would take on even greater loveability.

Attunement or empathy happens when an animal tunes into another's quality of energy and resonates with it. When one gets upset, animals can feel the anxiety because of the connection that they have with us. If the connection is close and trusting, it ties you together, just like a rope joining your hearts. When your emotions tug the rope, your pet feels the tugging and is pulled to you. This goes both ways. Whatever affects one of you affects the other.

When something is wrong, pets sense it and often choose to stay in tune with us until they figure out what is going on and how to help us. Then by resting their head on our lap or cuddling us, they show they understand and are tied to us. An animal's sensitivity is usually just a quiet, simple gesture that is so soothing and helps us. From a pet's connection comes a feeling of closeness and concern that is comforting and calming.

If people treat animals with the same love they would want for themselves, the animals have more heart and strength. Our love may give animals strength and the opposite is also true. When animals love and support us, we become stronger. There is a circle of love between our beloved pets and us. Tucker is the leader of this circle of love.

As soon as Tucker entered my life I started noticing that whenever I was tired or sad he would jump up on my lap and try to cheer me up. Tucker would notice if Cheyanne did not feel well and he would sit by her side. As time went on and more and more pets entered our lives I noticed that Tucker came to the rescue of each pet, not to mention person in his life. If a mishap came about, such as stepping on Emerald's tail, Tucker would come running to comfort Emerald. When Calum Sweeney cried out against going to the vet, Tucker stood watch until his return. If Eva ran into the screen door and let out a little "yep," Tucker would come running and make sure Eva was all right. When Apache would cry to be let outside to do his business Tucker would prance around the corner and made sure I was letting Apache out. When Penny's claws were stuck in the curtains, Tucker climbed up on the couch and tried to help Penny. If Zoe hissed because Eva got too close to her cat food, Tucker would come and be the peacemaker.

One day my friend came over and had an unusually loud sneeze that awoke Tucker from a deep sleep. Tucker ran toward my friend and leaped onto his lap and made sure he was fine. When my sister stubbed her toe and let out a loud yell, Tucker came to the rescue. Every sneeze, cough, and sigh, Dr. Tucker would come running. Each time a tail or paw was accidentally stepped on it was Tucker to the rescue, almost immediately, in super hero time!

One day as a cup crashed to the floor and glass shattered everywhere, Tucker ran to the rescue. I quickly picked him up saying "Not this time Super Hero, I don't want any glass to get into those precious paws." As I contemplated Tucker and his heroic actions I wondered if The Too Lovable Cat was also a Super Hero Cat.

Vicki Myron wrote a wonderful book about a library cat called <u>Dewey</u>. Only when Dewey was a few weeks old, on the coldest night of the year, he was stuffed into the returned book drop at the Spencer Public Library in Spencer, Iowa. Soon the library adopts the precious little cat and names the kitten, 'Dewey Readmore Books' or 'Dewey' for short. Dewey soon becomes a celebrity and rejuvenates the library. In her book, Myron mentions that Dewey's favorite hiding place in the library is between the Westerns on the bottom shelf. If Tucker was at the library I imagine he would hang out with the Super Heroes in the Graphic Novel Youth Section with the Batman, Iron Man, Superman, Wonder Woman, Xmen books and comic books. How lucky can I be to have not only a Too Lovable Cat, but also a Super Hero Cat!

# CHAPTER 20

## *Holy Cat*

*"If you, like me were made of fur and sun*
*warmed you, like me you'd purr."*
—*Karla Kuskin*

As my story comes to an end, it is siesta time in the house. Tucker, the too lovable cat, is asleep on my bed. He fell asleep next to my rosary, which he often does. Sometimes I find my rosary wrapped up in his little paws. When this happens I call him Holy Cat and wonder if he was deep in prayer. Animals with their simplistic and loving nature seem closer to the Divine. As I gaze upon my too lovable, holy cat sleeping, I think how lucky I am to have him as my friend. Then softly I say, as I often do when he first slumbers away, "Where is my Tucker"? He sleepily gazes up at me through slanted eyes and gives me that familiar coo followed by soft, gentle purring.

Emerald is snoozing on my mother's patio deck or should I say on the "PATTY O." My mother's maiden name is Patty O'Brien so our friend made a banister portraying the name, "PATTY O," my mother's nickname, in large letters in the hand railing leading to the gazebo.

Zoe is out in the garage on top of my mother's car, one of her favorite places. She has a bird's eye view of the world up on top of the car. She has a panoramic view of the neighborhood looking out all the windows of the garage.

The rest of the gang is stretched out in the living room. Cheyanne and Apache on the floor with the autumn sun glistening upon them. Eva and Penny on the couch with the sun beams streaming on them. With Angel and Aqua chirping softly in the background and Flip-Flop swirling around in his bowl, it is the perfect day. Or as Beatrix Potter said, "With pomp, power, and glory the world beckons vainly, in chase of such vanities why should I roam? While peace and content bless my little thatched cottage, and warm my own hearth with the treasures of home."

No matter what you call him—Taco Bell, TaaTaaTaaTaa, X-Files cat, Dr. Tucker, Super Hero, Holy Cat, the Too Lovable Cat, or just plain Tucker—he is one amazing, extraordinary cat and I can't image my life without him.

*"What greater gift than the love of a cat?"*
*—Charles Dickens*